SOUL JOURNEY TO LOVE

100 Days to Inner Peace

Irene A. Cohen, MD

BALBOA.
PRESS
A DIVISION OF HAY HOUSE

ISBN: 978-1-4525-5086-2 (sc)
ISBN: 978-1-4525-5087-9 (e)
ISBN: 978-1-4525-5088-6 (hc)

Library of Congress Control Number: 2012907230

Balboa Press books may be ordered through booksellers or by contacting:

Balboa Press
A Division of Hay House
1663 Liberty Drive
Bloomington, IN 47403
www.balboapress.com
1-(877) 407-4847

Because of the dynamic nature of the Internet, any web addresses or links contained in this book may have changed since publication and may no longer be valid. The views expressed in this work are solely those of the author and do not necessarily reflect the views of the publisher, and the publisher hereby disclaims any responsibility for them.

The author of this book does not dispense medical advice or prescribe the use of any technique as a form of treatment for physical, emotional, or medical problems without the advice of a physician, either directly or indirectly. The intent of the author is only to offer information of a general nature to help you in your quest for emotional and spiritual well-being. In the event you use any of the information in this book for yourself, which is your constitutional right, the author and the publisher assume no responsibility for your actions.

Any people depicted in stock imagery provided by Thinkstock are models, and such images are being used for illustrative purposes only.
Certain stock imagery © Thinkstock.

Printed in the United States of America

Balboa Press rev. date: 06/25/12

Preface

Soul Journey to Love is a book of inspirational messages, processes and prayers to bring all who so desire to be closer to Oneness and to what I have chosen to call God. The words in this small book came to me during my morning meditations from the fall of 2010 through the summer of 2011. I did not start out writing a book. I was only writing from my meditative state with the Voice for Love, which some might call the higher self or Holy Spirit. In the middle of October 2010 I was "instructed" to write daily as it would become a book and that it would be coming through me, not as dictation, but as a melding of me and that larger part of my Self. I had already been trained in how to hear this inner voice by taking a course in the Voice for Love taught by DavidPaul and Candace Doyle. But what I was experiencing went beyond that course of study and I felt definite promptings and directions to continue this project, including its editing entirely with Spirit rather than from my more mental and intellectual self.

About one-third into this book's writing I was also guided to stop reading spiritual books or listen to spiritual material except for continuing my second round of practicing the daily lessons from *A Course in Miracles*, a book of which I have been a student for several years. In this way I was told that my writing would be less affected by what I might be currently reading. Some of what you read here can perhaps be found in others' writings as well, but all is uniquely from my own voice.

The word God is used throughout the book. I am not referring to God in a strict Judeo-Christian sense, but rather God as portrayed in *A Course in Miracles*, a God of Oneness and unity with all, the God that is within us and in all things simultaneously, the loving Creator and Source; God as the light of consciousness.

I distinctly hear an inner voice in my mind but it often comes out as "We." This has been so from the beginning. I have decided that "We" refers to the small egoic self and the larger Self combined as one, but still with enough separation for me to not yet think of myself as fully One with God.

There was much transition in my outer life during the time of the book's writing—moving to a completely new environment for the first time in my life, my son's ongoing issues, job stresses—but, and as a consequence, I was less affected than I once used to be. For these issues I received many personal messages which are not included in this volume but which applied the book's principles. The messages in the book however were meant both for me and for others. However, I know that many of the entries about thoughts and fears are due to my own. In the end, the only fear we truly have is of being separate from God, which is the ultimate untruth.

Some background about me: I am a physician trained in psychiatry and in practice for almost 30 years. I was not brought up in a religious family but as secular Jews we observed some holidays, although we never went to synagogue. I explored my religious background briefly in early adulthood. Trained in voice, I sang Western liturgical music in choir performances which I enjoyed, but I did not feel a strong call toward a personal relationship with God nor did I embrace any one religion. Although I have meditated from the mid-1970's onward, I wished for but did not have a sense of that greater self which I could become until my study of qigong (Chinese meditative movement) in the mid-1990's. For several years thereafter I studied various esoteric topics in search of that Oneness with God which had heretofore eluded me. Each course of study I undertook opened me up more and more to this experience. I was also looking for ways to help my patients in whom traditional treatments seemed to have limited benefit, and as I learned, I passed on what I knew.

In 2004, while already on this path, I discovered that my then adolescent son had a substance abuse problem. This only spurred me on further to try to find inner peace and equilibrium, to learn to let go of my preconceived ideas and judgments and to know when to hold on and to be of help.

Although I am a physician, nothing in this book is offered as professional medical advice and indeed my more logical self is surprised at some of the suggestions that Spirit has given regarding health and healing. Please consult with a medical professional if you have a medical problem.

Acknowledgments:

I honor all my teachers who have helped me on this path back to my true self. In chronological order they are: Frank and Luke Chan, my first Chilel Zhineng qigong teachers; Fabien Maman who taught me about sound and color; Patricia Janusz, my true spiritual teacher, who could see the inner teacher within me; the teachings of *A Course in Miracles* which made me aware of a larger truth outside of the reality we think we know and DavidPaul and Candace Doyle who so simply taught me how to hear the Voice for Love. My greatest teacher however has been my son Seth and I acknowledge the loving acceptance of my husband and best friend, Michael.

Introduction

How to use this book:

This book is meant to be read and reflected upon as one passage a day for 100 days. If you wish, you can linger on a passage for more than a day. Do not read it all at once as the information builds upon itself with some repetition. You may also be intuitively guided to open to any page and know that it will be the right one for you. The choice is yours. If you feel that journaling your thoughts will help you, then by all means do so.

The book is divided into three parts. Part I contains general and specific instructions in how to quiet the mind and go within. Part II is more explanatory about the mind of God or universal mind and its relation to us and Part III is more lyrical, consisting of prayers and poems. These sections have some fluidity to them and you will find instructions in Part II, explanations in Part I and hopefully, lyricism throughout.

PART I

Day 1

In all things hold yourself true
And listen to your inner voice.

The thoughts you are thinking are not the true thoughts
of love and peace which are your birthright.

Underneath the toil and activity of your day is a stillness
within. Seek the way inward and you will find who you
really are.

This book will help you achieve this state. It is up to you
to continue its work.

Be vigilant about your thoughts, observe them, be loving
toward them and let them go.

There is a new universe within you which only you can
find. No book can take you there nor tell you what is there,
it is only your experience which will teach you.

Each has his own path on the soul's journey back to its
source of love.

Enjoy the ride.

Day 2

Your magnificence as a being is beyond compare. You hold the entire universe in your mind and heart. Your mind can be your friend or foe in case you have not figured that out yet. When you use the expression, I am of two minds, there is a deep knowledge within of which you are not even consciously aware.

Your mind is split between the habituated thought patterns that you have layered upon yourself from the time you could think, from what you learned from your parents, from school, friends, from society and the other mind.

The other mind is your true self, your true being. It has always been there. It is your unique energy signature but it is the part of you that is always connected to God. You hear this part of your mind talking to you when you watch a sunrise in awe, you hear this part of mind when you meet someone as if it is a coincidence, you hear this part of your mind, connected to something greater than you when you are at peace, sitting in a meadow, a church, a concert and you feel that all is well. This is a feeling you would like to have all the time.

But the first mind, the habituated mind, sometimes gets in the way of what we will call open mind. The habituated mind is full of details and worries, what ifs and what to do next. The habituated mind listens to the outside world and reacts to it. The habituated mind tells you that you will not do anything with your life, that you are ordinary and not good enough, that others are wiser, smarter, more handsome, thinner.

The habituated mind is an illusion, a fabrication of your thinking which comes from a distorted view of who you think you should be. As said before it originates in what others think about you and who you should be. And being the social animal that you are, you have complied.

However, this is not the truth about you.

The truth only lies within. In fact, you won't get it from a book. You will get it from going within yourself, from listening for the tiny stream that connects to the larger river of the universe, the river of God, so to speak. "How do I do this?" you say. "I live a hectic life, always going from place to place. I barely have time to sleep." And we say, you can slow down at any time you choose: in your car, on the bus or train, on the way to a meeting, in the quiet of a quick shower or a luxurious bath. You can slow down enough to listen to your open mind. It is always best if you can set aside time to go within, to meditate or reflect. But that is often not possible.

And so, if you find yourself walking somewhere alone, even if it is from one end of your workplace to the other, make it a meditation.

Walk and breathe in: I am walking, I am observing, I am living.

Walk and breathe out: I am alive, I am free, I am one with all.

Let the words come to you for your own walking meditation.

It is in the power of observing yourself just a little bit that you break free of the habituated mind. You can notice that you are overthinking or worrying and criticize yourself for it when you observe it. Or you can notice you are thinking in a habituated way and say to yourself, "I choose to let go of this and just be."

It truly is as simple as that. No more needs to be said.

Day 3

The letting go of thoughts and emotions is the most difficult for you. We do not say let go of all thoughts because it is through your thinking mind that you filter so much of what comes to you. We just ask that when you notice you are analyzing, judging, thinking, that you say to yourself, "I can stop now and be at peace." When you notice that you are fraught with unwanted emotions, you can turn to feelings of love and peace, to be loving toward every thought or emotion. This gives you permission to have the thoughts and to allow yourself to lay them aside.

The darker thoughts, which come from the habituated mind, arise and need to come to the surface. Like mist over a field on a cool day, the sun comes out and burns away the mist. So too does your own being, your inner being, allow those thoughts and emotions to arise and allows them to lift up and be taken away. Some call this turning it over to God or the Holy Spirit. If this is helpful to you at present, then use this phrase. The point will be to literally clear your mind as thoughts come up. So whether you are being loving toward those thoughts or turn them over to God, accept yourself and move on. There is no need to dwell on any one thought more than another.

The Buddhist teaching that thoughts have no meaning in themselves is helpful here. From where do thoughts originate? Are humans so unique that only we have thoughts? We are probably unique in that we have so many negative thoughts. These negative thoughts or cognitions are distortions, originating from habituated ways of thinking over and over again. They become distorted in our minds and are dwelt upon as if they have real meaning. However there is no real meaning we can truly give to our thoughts because how can we determine which thoughts are better or more important than others? There is no such thing. Thoughts are just thoughts, with no true meaning except that which we give them. Once we stop being so attached to the meaning of those thoughts, especially the negative ones that pull us in, then we can observe ourselves more and examine those thoughts for their validity. We are not saying that you should judge your thoughts. But you can ask yourself if those thoughts are really true.

If you go within to see if those thought are true, you will find that there is no real truth to any of them, neither the good nor the bad ones.

Better yet, go to that quiet place in your mind, even if you still have thoughts, and see how you feel. Invariably you will feel good or neutral or at peace. This is a sign of being more in tune with who you truly are, not with the thoughts.

You are not your thoughts. You are more than your thoughts. Your thoughts are a byproduct of experiences which you have decided to keep and hold onto and have become a distorted way of being. We love our cognitions and think they are so important. They are not that important. You will see as you read further how unimportant they are.

To become the observer of yourself and not judge it is the key to opening the path to go within and find out who you truly are.

Day 4

You can be still and at peace at any moment. It is a matter of paying attention to it, tuning into one radio station as opposed to the other radio station you have been playing. The open mind is always open to other communication. It is not hindered by external circumstances. It is not stopped by emotional difficulties.

The open mind is always open, always receiving from the One that is always communicating.

Day 5

In order to fully awaken, the mind must be clear. But to be in the world there are many things which cloud your picture of the truth. There is only one truth although many ways to get there. The final steps, however, are the same.

Think of it as if you are living in a parallel universe. There is the world that you live in, that you see. And there is another world, completely different, the true world, where everything is truly all right no matter what.

You begin to see everyone walking in the first world through the eyes of the other true world. The brilliance and light of who they truly are come into the forefront of your vision. You see the uniqueness of their energetic signature but you no longer are concerned about what they are saying, what they look like, how they are being.

You are seeing them as divine.

In conversation with a person, whether it be at work, at a shop or while at home, you see them as they truly are, a being of God, divine, as are you. You begin to see almost a halo around them, their auric field, and who they are as a physical body fades away. Walk around all day like this and you will feel "high" because you are unaccustomed to seeing them in their true state and you are not accustomed to being in yours either.

It is an exhilarating feeling at first. But you do not want to stay exhilarated. You want to train yourself to see all beings as their truth. This is the first step in the final steps to awakening.

Day 6

You are the most wondrous being on earth and in all the universe of your mind and beyond.

We are here to help you find the connection to your true self again.

We are here to let you know that you are never alone and that everything you do is part of a plan you created before creation in order to further your soul's growth.

All lessons in life are that. All supposed suffering is to show you where the path truly is. While you can just "be" and you think this is the existence you seek, just being is boring to you. You need contrasting experiences to temper the feelings of oneness. If all is One then there is no more.

So we say to you, cherish this contrasting experience and know that its purpose is for you to grow and learn, to let go of attachments and likes, to concentrate on the true love of your being, to not be aware of the wants and to concentrate on what your soul needs.

You need solitude but also others on your path. You need stimulation but also quiet. You need warmth but also the cold. See the contrasts and rejoice in them.

Day 7

In order to better explain these processes, think of the universe as a vessel but one without the usual boundaries. In it place all the thoughts and feelings that have ever been created. You are in the center of that vessel of consciousness and thoughts that come to you are not really always yours, but are manufactured from the universal extension of all thoughts placed in that vessel. If you are particularly sensitive you may find yourself having a lot of thoughts which are not even yours. But the human brain being what it is creates meaning and beliefs out of these thoughts. You are truly pure consciousness and the best way to rid the mind of thoughts is to gently acknowledge them from your heart in a loving manner and let go of them. It is when the thoughts become your beliefs that they become embedded in your psyche and your emotions come into play.

If you think of a thought as just a thought with no value of its own, it will not become a belief.

If you observe your thoughts you will see that many random thoughts, not necessarily connected to each other, come to you throughout the day. This is the mind just doing its job, picking up thoughts from here or there, from experiences you have had, seen, tasted, smelled, heard someone else talk about. Then your mind will bring into it associations of other experiences that are like the thoughts you had just been thinking. Thus it snowballs and belief systems begin.

If you want to be truly happy you cannot believe your thoughts. You have to believe that these thoughts are not yours to own and cherish. These thoughts are just the mind or ego wandering around and picking up bits and snatches from here and there.

Day 8

Only in a special relationship do issues between others really matter. If there is no specialness then there is no need for anything to matter.

If, for example, you feel that you must be a certain type of mother or your child must act a certain way, then it seems to matter. But in reality, it matters not. All is always well and will always be so. All has already happened.

It is not for you to figure out why and how certain things happen.

Each is on his own path. It is not for us to understand another more than we understand ourselves.

There is no need for worry or anxiety. You are accustomed to a feeling of anxiety as if you could know everything beforehand and that would solve all problems, which it does not. In the end, all that is real is the soul, the true self, and none of this intrusion of work, home, family, life. None is real. None is needed. You need no one nor relation with them. However, you choose your relationship with others. But you could also choose to see it in another way.

Day 9

It is good to look at your attachments, the relationships and things which you find special in your life because through the examination of attachments you see where your sticking points are.

If you are overly worried or attached to someone, it relates back to a worry within yourself.

If you desire someone to be different from the way he or she is, then the attachment is strong.

Your best and ultimately only attachment is to God.

You and God are not separate, you are One. You are not alone at any time, but asking for the answer is the key. Because you are attached to earthly concepts like your children, your spouse, your friends, your home, you have a stake in the world which is the way of fear.

If you can examine these and let them go, little by little, they will fade away in their importance to your worry, guilt and fear. You can see them from a more objective stance. For example, are your children truly your own? Or are they here with you a little while for you to care for them enough so that they can grow into their own souls and find their own soul's purpose? The experiences they are having are for their learning.

You are not the judge of them nor are you the master of another, so we say to gently let them go and see them for who they truly are, magnificent beings fulfilling their soul's purpose only for the experiencing of it. It is for them to process later or perhaps when they are no longer here.

Day 10

Although we are giving you steps, there are no steps to awakening. There is no one true path. There is only Oneness or separateness. Surrendering to the Oneness is the answer that you seek.

Look at your ego, that which you call your self. This is not your true self, but an apparition, a false self. It keeps within it all the hopes and dreams of this lifetime, all the sorrows and disappointments, all the rejections and anger, hatred, rivalries, wrong and right that you have experienced from the time of your birth into this physical body.

It is not real. It is not reality.

You are a distinct energetic signature of a larger whole. Sometimes you will feel you are that whole but most of the time when you walk around you don't feel that way, otherwise you would stop walking. Just the idea that you have somewhere to go could be considered separateness from God and, in a way, it is.

But if you understand that you have a unique energetic signature and that you seek experiences for the sake of your soul's greater understanding and for the expansion of that which is God, then all experiences are equal, none better than the other: the job you don't like, the man or woman who rejects you, the child who is going his or her own way. It is all the same as the joy you feel, the happiness you have, the desire to do interesting things or meet interesting people.

All experiences are the same. Not because they are not real, but because they just are that—experiences—which the soul is absorbing and taking in, without the whole, to compare with other souls and to enjoy.

It is not that the world is not real; it is that there is a greater reality. Those who want to renounce the world will be fine as well as those who wish to renounce the ego. It does not mean that your personality changes or you don't have likes and dislikes, preferences, as you would say. It is that all experiences become equal, no better nor worse than another. You can experience sadness on one hand, but also know that it is not the true you that is having the experience. You can think a negative thought and realize you are not the true thinker. These thoughts and feelings may be there for a long time but then they can fade away. It is a remembering and it is a forgetting, a remembering of the truth, a forgetting of what is not needed.

Day 11

You may be interested in physical healing. There are many theories which try to help you or explain to you how to heal.

Find a way of being in touch with the universe within and outside of you, to be able to connect with the peace and wisdom within. Some people must feel it is coming from outside themselves and for those people the healing comes through others.

To be in a position to heal, you must allay all fears. Work your way through the negative emotions to find the positive ones of acceptance, love and forgiveness of yourself and others for the way you feel either about yourself or about them.

In that space of Oneness with God, you can see yourself free of illness, be healed, be whole.

If the illness is serving some purpose and you no longer need it, then discover the purpose through self-inquiry and let go of it. Let it float away from you.

Illnesses will come and go. The more you think about an illness, the bigger it becomes. Turn it all over to God, the universe, your doctors and healers, and feel the best that you can.

Day 12

Today we will concentrate on being with others and still retaining the sense of self while being in communion with them.

You are all brothers cut from the same cloth. You are all a part of one universal consciousness. You will find that you retain your unique energetic signature but that you have more in common with your brothers than you do not. You all have one mind, even if it seems as though you are separated.

To enter into communion with another you do not need to give up your individual energy. You do not need to relinquish who you are. You need only be in conscious connection with your own inner source and guidance at all times. When you forget, remind yourself to go back to it.

When you forget, it is all right.

Just because you are in communion with others does not mean you take on their own energies. You are still yourself and you will always be yourself. This is not an illusion.

You are here for the greater experience, for you to be in a physical incarnation to interact with other souls in a physical manner—talking, laughing, crying, fighting, communing, joining, separating—because in the nonphysical realm the range of experience of emotions is not present. You are here to experience emotional situations and to gather your responses. There are greater lessons of your soul to learn and you will learn them through the manifestations you bring about in your daily life.

At some point you may feel a yearning or a pull to something greater than yourself. Then the awakening to who you truly are begins.

But at the same time you are still a human in physical form and as such you will retain beliefs, feelings and thoughts. These are not bad or wrong. They just "are." This is the way of the world, to have these expressions. When you continue to awaken you may have fewer of these intense experiences or fewer intense emotional reactions to them.

Sometimes you are born into a particular mindset for the purpose of working through an issue the soul has an interest in. There are those who are always anxious, or depressed, or angry and have been so since birth. These are souls have decided to have this intense experience to explore it in all its aspects and then to come to another conclusion. You may awaken from this experience during your physical time on earth or you may not.

It does not matter. It does not matter how far you get in this incarnation. One purpose of life on earth is to explore all the variety of these experiences and to feel them in a physical way. This is what you are here to do. And you have no choice, you are doing it. So enjoy the experience, both the bad and the good, for you have come here for this.

There is no karma, this is not a "do over," this is merely the chance to explore and experience. You may choose the difficult or the easy path. In the end it is all the same. Therefore, in a time of stress and strife you may find that you are having a negative experience you do not like. This is often the case with negative experiences. As such, look at them with the objectivity and the love that you have and relax. Close your eyes and see if an image or thought arises which does not appear to come from an emotional place. This will be the prompt to look at this situation or reaction through awakened eyes.

You will gain much from doing this exercise. You may do it daily. Go over events which have disconcerted you and see if something comes to you which will elucidate its purpose for your soul.

Day 13

You are moved at all times to have me speak through you. It is your inattention to the voice within rather than it not being present. You are able to tune in to this frequency at any time. You are able to hear the voice of God at all times. It is a matter of attention.

Train your mind to listen only for this voice. Train your attention to notice the other voice of your mind and then turn again toward God's voice.

It is all a matter of attention. Which one do you want to pay attention to? Your thoughts of worry, anger, daydreaming, any other emotion? How does it make you feel? Usually, not good. That voice is not from God. That voice is the one you have been listening to your entire life, but it is in error for what it says is not the truth. That voice is ingrained in you and like any habit, it takes time to stop it.

The other voice, the voice of God, is loving and positive. It is the voice of truth, of certainty, and it comes from within you as your own inner teacher. If you allow yourself to be guided by that voice of God you will never be led astray. You will never feel badly while listening to it and following its gentle guidance to go one way or another.

The voice of God is waiting for you with open arms. The door is open and you only need walk in.

Come.

Day 14

Oneness is achieved not from a longing for it but from a knowing that it can be.

Oneness is all there is. There is no more than that.

Know that you can achieve that sense of Oneness with all by just turning your attention to it and away from the worldliness around you.

In your everyday life, you can bring that sense of Oneness with all by preparing yourself beforehand.

Meditating at the beginning of the day to set yourself off on the right foot is the best way to begin.

Meditate on Oneness, on the unity of all things in this world and others.

Relax and feel within yourself the expansion of all within you and all the possibilities you hold.

Accept all thoughts that come to mind and release them. Go through them and allow them to pass through you.

Focus instead on the Oneness of all. When thoughts distract you return to your breath and the sense of Oneness.

Do not feel you need a mantra, a focus of attention. Accept all thoughts that come to you but treat them equally.

Become quiet, very still. And then allow your mind and soul to enter another place, another dimension.

Allow yourself to be transported to a place with no time, no sight, a blank black space where you sit and can receive.

If you wish to ask a question, you may. Or ask to be prompted by the divine for guidance. Or ask what is your purpose for the day.

Breathe quietly and listen within. It will be given to you, always and with great love.

The answers are always there within you. You must tune to the frequency in which to receive. You must know in your heart that you are open and that you can receive at all times.

When you start your day in this way you will be ready for all that comes your way and you will receive much guidance and loving kindness from your innermost being.

As the day goes on, remember the feeling of sitting alone and bring yourself back to it throughout the day even if you are very busy. Thus you will imprint upon yourself a way to be at all times, a way to allow one thought to follow the other but to treat them all equally. For they are nothing but thoughts and they are random even if you later try to make logical sense of them. These are not the thoughts to listen to. The other thoughts, the ones which are true, come from within, not from the mind you know, the mind with which you are familiar.

The thoughts that are true come from a deeper place within you which you can access at any time, but it takes practice to allow them to come to the fore.

Go within at all times and be refreshed. Be renewed. Be at peace. Be at One with all.

Day 15

You are love and light and this is all that you have ever known. You are floating on the precipice of here and there. You are non-judgment. You are love.

The living embodiment of love is to give everything that you have without expectation.

The living embodiment of love tells us to freely love without conditions, without expectations, without disappointments or grief. Without anticipation, without any of the worldly attributes that one usually associates with love: jealously, hurt, abandonment, fear, loss, happiness in the arms of the beloved, wiping away the tear of a child. This is not the love that you seek.

You seek something deeper and more abiding. You seek a love that can be unshaken by outside events, catastrophes, life, death, anything you think affects you from others or from circumstances.

You seek a love that is greater than all.

It is the love of God and it encompasses all other little loves. It is the permanent opening of the heart, an opening which brings with it the amazing light and love of the universe.
It is the love that you seek in the quiet times and in the desperate times.

You have this love right now. Right here. You no longer need to seek it.

Be still and it will seep into every pore of your being. You will be light and love. You will be able to see through the detritus of others' supposed difficult lives and love them only for who they are. You will see that you can love all equally no matter what they might do. You will see that you have the abiding love of God with you at all times and that you can share this love with all who come your way.

And in this way the healing for you and the world continues. It has never stopped. All the "brokenness" of people is an illusion, the beggar and the billionaire. They all have the unending love of God, as do you.

Your power of love, which is not yours alone, will heal all the world.

Day 16

Think not that you are unloved in any situation in which you judge yourself. A good way to step outside your mind is to think of yourself as an observer only. Watch yourself go through the motions of a simple action, like making a cup of coffee. Then you can apply that power of observation to your mind's thinking.

At each step of thinking, step back and say, "What is this? Does this serve my true purpose?" And you will see that it is not so, that you are not serving your truth by the way you are thinking. Your thinking is probably full of judgments on various levels but each of the judgments leads you away from God, not closer. So we say to you to stop and observe the thinking and when you notice it, turn toward God.

You may do this by asking a question like that of Ramana Maharshi, "Who am I?" Or you can be loving to those thoughts at every moment. You can recite a mantra to give you a point of focus. Or you can just turn and turn again to God, not to thoughts of God but to God itself. Just turn to God, turn your face away from what ails you and seek your comfort in God. You will always be rewarded.

Day 17

Wake up in joy.
That is your aspiration.
Even if you do not like your life at present.
Wake up and be joyful and grateful anyway for another day on earth.
Wake up with the sun and see it love the earth as it does.
Wake up and be present at all times.
It is helpful to watch the mind and not allow it to stray.
It is helpful to meditate first thing in the morning. Be quiet and still and say nothing. Then spend some time with yourself and God before your day begins.

In silence all things are revealed.

No fears need be there. All is always truly well for you and everyone.

There is always a way to solve any problem, but not by taking action, not by running and doing. Just let it be and it will resolve itself on its own.

Day 18

Be still at all times, even when moving.
"How do I do that?" you say.
By noticing the mind and quieting it.
By noticing that the mind is chattering this way and that and saying to yourself, "Be still an instant."
Be still an instant. How long is an instant? As long as you want it to be. An instant can be imperceptible or it can last forever.
Notice at every moment if you are thinking of other things while doing something else. Think of nothing else but what you are doing.
I am typing.
I am washing my face.
I am washing dishes.
I am eating.
I am driving.
When other thoughts intrude, go back to what you are doing.
This puts you in the present moment only and always.
And that is all you need for enlightenment, being at peace in the present moment.

Simple, isn't it?

Day 19

We will speak with you today about fear.

Fear is part of separation from the whole. Fear is a primal animal feeling which is supposed to be part of your physical survival mechanism. However, in your Western world, survival is rarely an issue. You will see that fear is more related to your mind and to separate ways of thinking. There is truly no reason to fear anything because you are an eternal soul always connected to the mind of God. It is the forgetting of this which allows fear to fester inside you. You note that the fear exists within you and then you label it with meaning. Rather we would say to you that you need fear nothing and trust everything to God. It is the inability to let yourself go and trust that creates fear.

Know that God is with you and with everyone at all times. The fears that arise are but imaginations. The ego can be very strong and this is one way it reveals itself. Always turn toward God, thoughts of God and God's protection when fear begins to come upon you and you will turn fear into flowers.

Day 20

You are pure love and devotion.
In everything you do and think, be love, be devoted to love and to the love of God.
It is not hard. Not as hard as you think.
It is a choice and it is the only choice.

Think only of love.
Think only of Oneness.
When you find your mind distracted by the world, stop the thinking. It takes an observant mind, that is all.

You should have something to think toward not something to think away from.
You can do this by applying your mind and observation powers. You can just turn toward God at every moment that you think of it.
You can see the love of God in every leaf, every turn on the highway, every interaction with others. You can choose to see God in everything at all times.

Take time today to observe your mind as often as you can. When you notice it straying, turn again to God. That is all you need do and nothing else. There is no magic in this. There is no need for years of study and devotion. It is a simple thing.

You are thinking. You notice yourself thinking.
Do not stop and think, why am I thinking about that?

Just think of God. Smile. Love.
And you will be, in an instant, in his loving arms.
It is so simple but so easy to forget to do.

Day 21

Question:
Why is there still suffering if we know we are eternal beings?

Answer:
There is still suffering because in your mind, the little "i," you see yourself as separate. You fall away from your true self and become small and alone.

Even if you have felt all alone before, you are not truly alone. Even if you feel the suffering of others, this is your choice. Any time you feel the suffering of others, know that you are not seeing them as their true identities and that they are just disguised eternal beings.

Any time you feel badly for someone else, know that you are looking at them erroneously and that you are not able to see past the blockages that you present to yourself. You prevent yourself from seeing them for the masters that they truly are.

Practice seeing the light in everyone, the light in all, the light that shines through no matter what the circumstances. Then you will be free of fear, free of suffering and you will be able to be in the joy of life's moment. Practice this light within yourself and others for whom you feel pain. That is the true compassion that you can give as a human in this worldly form.

Day 22

You are learning that you must trust: trust your guidance and trust in God. There is truly nothing else but this. Go within quietly and listen to your true self. This can be done in quiet or not. Just remember to do so.

All is truly well. The angels of God look down upon you and all whom you worry about and we say there is no need for worry, ever. It will be revealed to you little by little how to awaken from your slumber here on earth by going through what you consider to be trials and tests. They are just gentle lessons to prod you into awakening. So do so gladly and the rewards will be One.

Day 23

How to hear the Voice of God even if you are upset

It seems true that when you are in a strong negative emotional state, you may feel cut off from God's voice or even from God's love. When this is the case, you may feel that you need God the most, but he is not there at all.

This condition is easily remedied.

God is always there, behind the door you have closed. You just have to open it.
God is always ready with love and guidance.
When you are in despair, think, "What would God do now?"
When you are in despair ask, "What should I do now?"
When you are in despair and desperation ask, "Is this the true me who feels this way or is this some other form of me who is at the fore right now?"

Keep questioning until you become so confused with your thoughts that you give up thinking your own thoughts. For your own thoughts are not worthwhile and are not necessary.

So think, "What would God have me do now?" Keep asking until you are a little at peace and get an inkling of an answer. It can be through a sign, a person, a book, a conversation, not always or even usually through a direct voice in your head telling you what to do. But you have to listen and look out for it. You have to be open to it.

So ask the question, "What am I to do now?" And listen for the first answer that comes without judgment. The answer can be as simple as "Just keep going." It will always be a positive answer.

Any negative answer like, "I am weary of living. I do not want to be here any more," is not coming from God. It comes from the ego, the habituated mind, not from the right mind, the mind of God.

God reaches out to you at every instant that you turn toward him but you often are turned away. Just by stopping and asking what should I do now, you will get your answer.

Trust in this.

It will always work and pull you out of the depths of your emotion and into the help and comfort you seek. God always loves you. And within yourself you always love yourself, no matter what you think you may have done or not done, no matter what you feel guilt about. It is always all right.

Day 24

You are learning to not pay so much attention to your thoughts and to instead focus on the inner peace of your heart and inner being.

You see that only you can generate peace and no one else. You can notice for yourself when you feel you are in calm waters or not. But you do not need to have the waters be calm. You can create it yourself especially with your thinking.

The key to all of this is love.
Not the anxious love of worry.
Not the cloying love of a lover who is afraid he will lose love.
Not the love that grasps and needs and wants.
But the unconditional love for all equally. The love which creates a positive experience within you and without you. The love that others can feel in your presence. You are able to exude this love because you know you want to stay connected to the love of God. And that you always have God's love at all times.

Just turn, turn again toward God's love and you will heal the world.

Day 25

You are wondering, always wondering what is next. But we say that you will never know. The infinite possibilities you see and the calamities that you fear are the same. There is no way to know anything without trusting that you will be guided in every step. Until you see that you are not in charge, your running here and there will be for naught.

Therefore we say that at every turn in the road you should turn toward God and ask what you should do. Ask what is his plan for you. For it is truly your own plan from within your inner self but you know it not. You think that it is your plan but you have no real plans on your own. That is from where your dissatisfaction emanates.

So we say be calm, clear your mind and just ask the question, "What is the next step? Should I do anything or nothing now?" And if you listen you will always hear the words or see the signs that you need.

Giving up your own way of thinking and doing is hard after all these years. But it is the only path to peace, to find yourself, to quiet your mind and be still as you follow your inner guidance which is infallible and will never lead you wrong. As you open up more to guidance, you will be with God more and you shall see how happy you are no matter what the circumstance.

Day 26

We come to you today to give you the peace of God. It is attainable if you turn toward God and away from your thoughts. It is attainable if you look at your thoughts in a new way and see that they do not mean you harm or good, but are manufactured habits that you have been thinking all along. They have no meaning in and of themselves. Just as your emotions do not have meaning either, they only have the meaning you put your attention on.

The way to relegate these thoughts to where they belong is to find the space between the thoughts, the holy place where no thought exists, the mindstream below the babbling brook of thoughts where you truly abide. Listen for this stream, it underlies all. It underlies all of life. This stream is where you truly think, you truly are one with all and it is from this stream that you want to deeply drink.

Go to that stream whenever you find your thoughts running away with you.

Go to that stream and see it as the stream of all life at all times.

Think of that stream and jump into its cool refreshing waters whenever you are too hot from all the thoughts that crowd your brain.

And there you shall find true peace.

Day 27

How to be happy, whole and complete

We are offering you something big by giving you this title and yet it is true. You can be happy, whole and complete. One answer lies outside of yourself and one within.

The answer outside yourself is to see nothing as it appears but as you see it in your mind. Your mind and God's are one.

To see nothing as it is, turn toward the world with God's eyes, the loving eyes of the parent who loves his child no matter what he does, who thinks his child is the greatest creation that ever existed. This is the way to see the world and everything in it, to bring to it only love. To bring to it only a sense of peace. To bring to it a sense of knowing.

Know that everything is as it should be in this moment and that the suffering, longings and judgments will work themselves out in the end. Love everyone and every thing and think not on the supposed harm that man does to man or, as you see it, man does to his planet. Everything is in perfect harmony and yet it looks as if it is in flux. This is because it appears to be constantly changing while underneath, at all times, it remains the same as it ever was.

The second answer is the true answer because it lies within. Take time every day to be with yourself and look within with quiet contemplation. This must be done no matter what else you do. To reach your true self, your guidance and the truth within, you must quiet the mind enough to let all things just be. And in that quieting you will find your true self. If it helps to write it down then do so, but it is not necessary. What is more necessary is to make contact with your true self and see that it is everlasting, eternal, always has been and will be. It will always be with you throughout all your lifetimes and in between, a consciousness you will always recognize as your true self.

So unpeel the layers of the world a little and allow that true self to come out and shine through. This can be done at any time, especially in the morning and at all times that you can remember. Include in this the times you are speaking and interacting with others because this is when the true self can join with others, which is really just one large self. In this way wonderful healing interactions can occur.

Day 28

You are One with the universe. There is no other way. All the strivings, longings, fears and defeats, the tearful nights, the joyous days, are expressions of being One. All feel these emotions and are joined. There is nothing else. There is only you and you alone.

Do not be in fear because in being you, the small self is not alone. The idea of being alone is a fallacy. This is something most have experienced and it is a cutting off of the energy of the life source. It is a fabrication of the mental and emotional state you can find yourself in.

Just be and abide. Within you is great wisdom. Knowledge is unimportant here.

Think of it like the ocean. It flows in, it flows out and recedes.

Let the waves of conscious being be like the ocean. The thoughts come in, the thoughts go out.

Feeling the presence of Oneness, the presence of your true self comes in and it goes out.

Pay attention to when the presence of Oneness comes in and pay attention to the thoughts going out.

In that period between the thoughts going out and the presence of Oneness coming in you will find your true peace, where no thought exists and you are free.

Day 29

You are wondering how to have no judgments in the world and still have perspicacity and discernment. These are not mutually exclusive. To have no judgments does not mean to not use your judgment. It means to not label anything good, bad, like, dislike, nor pay attention to the thoughts that follow those labels.

But you need to use good judgment, so to speak, to know not to cross the road when a car is coming in your way, to be useful in your line of work and so forth. You can ask God to guide you in all those things but the idea of good judgment is just that—you know that God would not guide you to cross the road into oncoming traffic, so there is no need to ask what you should do. The instincts are intact but the thought pattern is what needs changing.

When you judge another or yourself, you can only feel badly thereafter. This is not communion with the Oneness of God. Notice at every step when you are using judgment against yourself and ask for guidance to give up the judgment. The noticing is the hardest part. Giving up the judgment afterwards is not difficult.

If you find resistance to giving up judgment then there is a belief that you are holding onto which should be examined and transformed. For example, the belief that a child should obey his mother. This is a belief and nothing else. The belief that people should act a certain way is another belief which becomes a judgment and which then leads you astray from your one true purpose, oneness with all. Make note of when it happens throughout the day and you will see how many times the mind will wander into judgment. There is no purpose to these judgments except to feel badly.

You can let them go. You will be able to allow yourself the peace of God in the letting go of all judgments.

Day 30

You are always at One with God. This is something to recall at all times especially when you seem to be forgetting. God is always with you because you have God within you and you are indeed of God. If everyone thought this way there would be less conflict in the world and in the inner world of many.

"Be still and know that I am God." No truer words were ever spoken. This is why they have so much meaning whenever they are said and thought.

You can never escape God, you can never escape being of God. There is no way and so it is futile to try.

Take time daily to remind yourself that God is always with you, even if it seems unbelievable. Your thinking cuts off this connection as does your strong emotional sense. Soothe yourself and know that God is within you at all times, gently giving you guidance and direction, knowing that all is as it should be and as it will be.

Day 31

Let your mind rest now.
No need to think about the world you seem to see.
No reason to go on in the way you have been doing.
Just rest.

Put your thoughts away and let your mind drop down into the ocean of love.
Let your mind fade from your conscious being and just be.
Be with yourself. And in that being still, you will find yourself and your relationship with God.
That you are pure and holy and nothing can take that away.
That no thoughts or actions you seemingly do can negate who you truly are.
That no condemnation, by yourself or others, can strip away your truth which is God's truth.

You can be at one with yourself by being at one with God.

Day 32

Have no fear for the future.

You wonder how this can be possible.

Fear is created only in your mind. Look at your fears: of dying, of those you care about dying, of having not enough money, of being humiliated, of being unworthy. None of those fears come from outside you. Those fears are manufactured by you and keep you imprisoned in your mind.

To overcome the fears you must examine them one by one, not only for their illogical qualities but because they are meaningless when placed side by side against God. They have no meaning to God and as you are truly one with God, they really have no meaning to you.

As fears arise, allow them their space, look at them and then turn away. Do what you need to do—turn it over to God, pray, live with the fear and let it dissipate on its own. Do all this, for you know that there is no fear in the realm of God.

You know in your heart that this is true even if fear feels very real. We say that you can acknowledge your fear while still knowing it is not true and not real. You can bow to it and bow away from it.

Fear does not originate from the truth that is you. Fear comes from another place, another mind, another habituated way of thinking that has been with you throughout this lifetime but which you see is unnecessary now. You can be free of fear. You can be free of your mind. Turn your thoughts to God who has no fear. You will be protected and safe, as you already are.

Day 33

All love is perfect.
All are perfect.
Just as they are.

Forget the faults and flaws of others for they do not matter.
Forgive the seeming mistakes of others for there are no true errors.

Each soul finds its way to the same home, the same God who is love.

Great masters disguise themselves as the poor, the drug addicted, the beggars,
But their souls are here just for that experience and leave them be for the expansion that they seek.

Know that God is in every one of them.
And that they are truly free, within and without.

Day 34

When I close my eyes,
I sink into the no-thing-ness of my being
And I am still.
A thousand worlds within worlds open up to me
As I listen for the silence
And become One with it.
It is true peace.

This is my practice
It nourishes and it receives
It takes me inward and it takes me away
But I am always here
Eternally.

Day 35

Breathing

When you focus on your breathing, there is nothing else.
Go into breath and if distracted, count the breaths for it
will bring you back to the moment, back to yourself.

You cannot concentrate on anything else in your mind if
you concentrate on your breath.

Sinking deeper into meditation, to the place of no-mind,
Find silence and peace.
And eventually you find that
Breathing is optional.
There is no need to breathe.

Day 36

At all times, try to have no thoughts.
Try this all day long, even as you are doing work which involves thinking.
Try to have no thoughts at all which are about the little "you," for you in this context do not exist.
Open yourself up to your internal wisdom and share it.

This is your practice, this is your birthright. It will come to fruition.

First stop the thinking and just be.
Be with yourself, be one with yourself.

That is all there is.

Day 37

The idea of having no thoughts, no personal thoughts seems easier than doing it.

Your thoughts come and go but it is in the catching of them and truly letting them go that you are free. Free to be who you truly are.

As you notice these thoughts, turn to no thought. It is easier than you think. This brings a peace which is hard to know otherwise. Know that love will see you through all of this process and there is no right or wrong in performing this task.

Let the thoughts arise. Let the thoughts go.

Notice you are having a thought. Have no thought. Be silent.

In time you will see there are fewer and fewer thoughts that arise.
There are fewer ideas that come to your mind.
There are fewer "trains of thinking" that you will have.
There are fewer unnecessary thoughts in your head.
And with this comes perfect peace.

Day 38

To develop your inner vision you must first stop paying attention to the outer world, including your own thoughts about the world and yourself.

It is good to sit in meditation at the beginning of the day so that you can quiet your mind and begin to hear your inner voice.

Your cares and fears will fall away as you settle down into the peace of God that is known to all the great sages.

Day 39

Question:
To give yourself totally to Me, who is Me? Who am I?
Who is the self to give up?
I do not know these answers.
What is the answer when I feel I am in my body, mind and emotions?

Answer:

Just think for a minute of your release, release from your ability to see through all this. Your awakening is a gradual process although you would like it to be sudden. Although there are times you feel you cannot bear it, you can and you will in joy and lovingness. Just see your thoughts for what they are and you will see how easy it is for you to discard them.

You will see how easily the thoughts mean nothing.

Day 40

Question:
When will peace come?

Answer:

The world and you are undergoing an evolution, a large transition. You will find peace within yourself, without death or illness, and you will find it now. It does not matter what circumstance you are in. The time of large contrasts is ending. You will see that in your own holiness lies the power of God. Trust in this.

Like all who seek and find, awakening seems gradual but at the end it is a quantum leap, one day it is there. You are being led to the right places and teachings to accelerate your awakening. You have learned that you can separate yourself from what you do in the world and still be happy and content. This is what you seek. You see that this is possible.

You know that for yourself love is the way and the answer.

Know that you are guided in everything you do.

PART II

Introduction To Part II

This is the last day of the introduction on how to be wholly one with God. These past 40 lessons set the stage for the next group.

You will be instructed on many ways in which the universe and God's principles play out in the world and in your mind. This will be different from the way you have perceived them before.

You will see that what you experience is of a whole, an entirety of the universe within and without and that many questions and mysteries can be solved, so to speak, by paying attention to these teachings. This is the next stage of illumination which you seek.

We suggest you set aside a period of meditation daily, even if brief, in order to be in a state of mind where you can allow God to work through you. This is not difficult.

Any of the exercises from the previous 40 days of instruction can help you. We suggest that you pick one and stay with it for a few days, but the way of picking one may be different from the way you are used to. Instead of leafing through the book or starting at the beginning, become still and quiet and let an inner nudging, an inner prompting come to you and allow that inner place to choose which practice might be best for you. It will always be the correct one.

You will see with practice that these processes will work on you profoundly although it may seem subtle at first. Some of you will have striking experiences and some will not. It matters not because everyone returns to God in their own way and in their own time.

Day 41

You are divine
And the divinity of those who come into your presence is always apparent.
Know that God's voice is your voice,
There is no other voice.
Anything else is false, a dream, a fabrication.
There is only one. One sound, one word, one life.
There is none else.
When you look upon the divine presence, when you think of it or are in its light,
You know the truth of what truly is.
You know in your heart and soul that there is only one truth, the truth of God's love.
The holy love that envelops you and every sentient being.
The love that creates worlds.
This love is so strong that it shines through every veil, every mountain, every dense and heavy place.
This love sustains the world and goes with you wherever you go.
This love is available to you at all times, no matter what circumstance you seemingly find yourself in.
Because there is none else.
There is only this powerful love of God.
This was the beginning, it is the middle and it will be the end.

Day 42

The world was created in an instant, not in millennia, not in seven days.

The world as you know it began in the mind of God and in the offshoots of that mind for the embellishment of their thinking. The wanting and knowing of those offshoots played with the ideas of physical form until the perfection of all that is in the world—from rocks to humans—was created.
The world is here for your experience of it, to be in the physical form in which you find yourself, to expand into it and beyond.

You have been in many worlds, sometimes simultaneously. We know this is hard to understand, but there truly is no time. This world is here for you to fully experience your emotions and your mind. Other worlds are more physical, or more psychical, or more mental. This is the one that is emotional. This is the one that is most unlike your true self and that is a challenge.

Your purpose, aside from joy, is to integrate your experience here with the experience you once knew, that experience of God, of Oneness, of unity, of being at one with all. Of being the mind of God.

Your true purpose is to return to the source. How you get there is what free will is about. There is no other free will than that, the journey to love.

Day 43

Healing and Illness

Healing comes from the mind. Illness also comes from the mind. Imbalance in the mind and emotions can lead to illness. The balance of both leads back to healing. Let your physical healing occur with your doctor, but it is the emotional and mental healing that we would like you to concentrate on.

Once a thought gets hold of your mind, or a shock to the system leads you to feel imbalance, usually in strong negative emotions or in thinking about something rather than letting it go, illness can occur. If the thought continues or the negative emotion continues the illness can develop in the body.

Have no fear. The good news is that God's light shines on all these apparent problems. In meditating and bringing oneself to wholeness again, the happy mind is the cure.

Can there be no illness if one is unhappy?
This is a good question and depends on the thought patterns of the particular person and what their soul also came to experience. Some souls have come to experience deep unhappiness and then find their way joyfully home. Some

souls may want to experience illness for their own growth and knowledge.

Rejoice at all times, even when unhappy. Because no matter how and no matter what, we are all going home. We will all get there. And so it matters not how one does it.

When confronted with illness, be in your right mind and think thoughts of love as much as you can. Do not let the small things bother you and you will see that you will have what you wish. Your body is perfect as is your mind.

God's light shines through despite what you feel or do. Turn toward the light and it will be apparent.

Be guided to act on what you are willed to do and it sometimes leaves as mysteriously as it arrived.

Day 44

You yourself may notice too much when you feel unwell. This in itself leads you more toward the ill feelings than the well ones.

Notice, acknowledge and let go. Notice, turn it over at all times, and let go. Do not count the number of things wrong with you. As with a passing pain, often as soon as it comes it will go.

This is the way of the mind and the body. First in the mind, not noticed. Then in the body, noticed. As we said before, keep a happy mind.

If the mind is unhappy, acknowledge it and move toward changing your mind. You may not succeed at all times but you will let go of it little by little.

Do not upbraid yourself for your thoughts. Do not make too much of your thoughts. Do not make too much of your sensations. Always seek out help from others if you feel you need it.

Do not ignore, but most importantly, just acknowledge and notice.

Day 45

The power of the mind

In giving all up to your higher power or higher self you will become more intelligent. You do not need to think so much because the inner wisdom which already is within you will do the thinking for you.

All book knowledge is stored within an energetic imprint in the universal energy. If you want to know something that has been already written or thought then you can tap into this universal library.

You know this is true when you have inspiration. For example, if you are a writer, sometimes the writing just flows through you and seems to not come from you, from your mind. Indeed it does not come solely from your mind for you are merged with the energy of the universe and the thoughts you are supposedly having are coming from a melding of your mind with the universal mind. In this way your unique energy imprint will be upon what you create in a way that no one else can do, borrowing from and molding the information available from the universal energy of which we speak.

It is not difficult to do this. All you need do is ask from a meditative state for help in this regard and you will receive the information that you need. This can be particularly important during times of testing, examinations, school writing, work projects or in teaching others on any type of subject. Just go within and merge with the universal mind.

The energetic imprint of all thoughts that have been thought, all books that have been written, all information from higher sources is available to everyone if they are tuned in to the right frequency. Worries and anxiety, anger and strong emotions can cause interference with tapping into this energetic flow. There truly is no need to study hard and read many books unless you so desire. If you try this you will be amazed at what you can accomplish. You may seem to be smarter than you were before. But what is actually occurring is the ability to merge with the universal mind where all is possible and known. This is free for everyone. It is encouraging that more and more are coming to this conclusion and utilizing this experience for the good of all.

Think of thoughts as energetic markers floating in space. These markers stay in their floating state until someone thinks a thought about them and asks for some help, clarification or information. That person's individual thought attracts that floating marker and the information in the marker will flow through the person's energetic body and into their thinking mind so that they can experience and know it.

Day 46

How to be led by your higher self

The way to be led is to listen at all times for any and all hints, signs and prompts to put aside your own thinking and take up your true nature. You will never be led astray. You will only find peace in this manner. There is only one way to truth and this is the way.

You may allow your thoughts to arise, but pay them no mind. Then you will see that they have no meaning on their own except the meaning that you give them. Just as you can be led to write without thinking beforehand so shall you lead yourself through the day. You can have two opposing thoughts in your mind but choose to listen to only one. You know how to quiet your mind therefore try to do this as much as possible.

In all things you do, feel that you are blended with your higher self who is the true you. You will see that it becomes easier and easier to be that one which your heart desires.

Day 47

Today we will speak with you about ways to not be separate from others. It is your separate thoughts, the ideas you have of being separate beings, which bring you the most suffering.

We say that your view of suffering is also incorrect, because you have a belief that suffering is real and that it is part of being human on earth. This is not the case but is a fallacy that your mind would like you to believe.

You and another have no separation except by your physical perception. In the realm of the spirit all are united, although each has its own energy which remains for all lifetimes and beyond. Your choices from the level of the soul allow you to have the experiences your body and mind are having today. How this plays out is what is called "free will."

You are not here to be separate beings, but to see yourself in others and to be of help to each other. It does not mean that you take on the burdens of others as your own and feel as badly as they feel. Rather, it means recognizing yourself in others no matter what they look like or how they act toward you or others. We are asking that you relinquish what you consider to be judgment because that judging comes from your mind and not from your soul. On the level of soul there is no difference.

There are great masters and teachers who have walked on earth and taught these same ideas but few have been able to truly hear them and implement what they asked. Why is this so? Because the belief in your own mind rather than the universal mind is what stops you from seeing the truth. If you suspend your judgments you will see the world through different eyes and you will act differently. It is the strong belief in being an individual, being separate, that stops you from seeing the All in humanity and the One in All.

Dissolving that belief will bring you true happiness.

Day 48

Fear and anxiety are only in the mind of the one who makes it. The origin of fear is from your thoughts, although it may at first seem to come from outside you.

Know that you are always with God and in this way fear is never true. It cannot be true because it is a fabrication of your mind. You will know when it is true: when you face a lion face-to-face, when you face a gun or a knife. That is what fear is meant for, to mobilize you to move away if you so choose.

But the fear of the mind, the anxieties and worries of the "what ifs," are what twist your emotions and thoughts.

You can discard fear knowing that the loving God would not allow such harm to come to you, that all your experience is what you choose and that you can choose again and again, not to feel badly, but to feel well.

The choice is always yours. Anxiety may be present but it need not overcome you. Fear may be present but you still can feel at peace.

Day 49

Fear is only the fear of death. There is no other fear that people truly have. There cannot be any other fear but the ones subsumed under this fear of annihilation of what you love so much, your life.

But there is no true death. You will of course see what you want to see after your body dies, but know that the only thing that is real is the eternity of your soul. Eternity is something you will glimpse throughout your life, but you long to know that you and those you love will not perish.

You will always be "here" wherever that may be. You will always be present. You will always have the consciousness of who you are, one with the whole, but with a recognition which is your own. You will be at peace, there will be no turbulent emotions.

And so we say you can have that now on earth in this lifetime. You can have peace, the peace of mind, the peace of your emotions fading into the distance, the peace from thoughts which are no longer needed.

You do not need to figure anything out because it is all perfect just as it is. Just be, and be present. You shall see this is enough for the end of fears. Witness your thoughts and pay them no mind. Let your mind join only with God and you will be free of fear forever.

Day 50

Fear is only in the mind. Once fear is overcome, infinite possibilities will open to you. The manifestation that many speak of is truly due to letting go of fear and allowing all possibilities to be directed by the mind and the mind of God. A blending, melding of the mind is one way to receive. Another way is to be guided in every step, trusting that all will be provided for.

The universe and God provide for everyone who is open to it. You must be in a state of receiving. You must feel that you are open, ready, with no encumbrances. You must trust wholly and totally in the divine guidance you receive and not look back, but only move forward on your path, even if you do not know what it is or what it is for.

The hand of God is in everything you do if you allow it. You can block it through your negative thoughts, negative emotions, doubts and fears.

Once fear is no longer there, the possibilities are laid out for you. Choose them with the guidance you receive. Choose them by asking what you should do if you do not know how to clearly receive the prompts which are offered to you. When there is a resounding "yes" it is easy. But occasionally you will be undecided and this is from the ego mind. Let that go and trust that you will be guided to the correct decisions always.

The origin of the abundance of the universe is from the mind's thoughts, the universal mind's thoughts of all that people want. This is elaborated in many books and teachings so the mechanics of this do not need elucidation here. Just know that you can have everything you want while you are in the world and that it is not a thwarting of your spiritual development to want and have things that will better your experience on earth, "the happy dream." While here there is no reason to not enjoy what the world offers. Know however that this is not all that there is. This is where the human race has become stuck, thinking that the pursuit of things and experiences is all there is.

All experience is good, the experience of lack and the experience of having. These experiences enhance your soul's journey and expand the consciousness of all and of God. There is no bad or good experience. It just is as it is. Accept it for whatever it is and learn from it, move on from it to the next experience.

Know again that the loving hand of God is in everything, if you ask for God. That is what you should ask for the most: for God to be with you in a way you can know and then all will always come to you. Your ego is the only block.

Know today that you can receive and trust in all things and you will be led to that which is truly yours.

Day 51

The eternality and infinity of you is the only truth you need to know.

The eternal truth is that your soul lives on before and beyond this physical incarnation, always seeking new ways of experiencing for its ever-present expansion.

The infinite truth is that you are, right now, in connection with all other beings, with all of the universe and beyond your concept of the universe, that as you sit here in this physicality of the earth you also have expanded outwards into the infinite reality of Oneness, of all, of God. You are as large as the universe and as small as a speck of dirt. You are truly part of and one with everything and yet it is often so hard to see.

There is an individual you, but not the "you" of the ego. The individual you is an energetic outpouring, an outgrowth of the larger eternal energy, the eternal soul of God. There are many ways to put it but the truth remains that there is no difference between the "you" that you experience and the God that you think is outside of yourself. It is all one and as such it is indivisible. Yet your own part of the larger soul wants to have certain experiences that other parts of the soul are not having right now and therefore you are in this body, in this physical incarnation on this planet at this time. It is simple but your thinking mind makes it very complicated. It is not complicated.

All day you can be in communication with the inner knowing of your eternity. You will see that you choose to incarnate, you choose where to incarnate, you choose which planet on which to incarnate. You have had millions of experiences and each one expands your vision and your soul's purpose, leading to the expansion of all other souls and to the larger whole. Your experience leads to the expansion of the universe itself and the expansion of that greater consciousness of which you are part. You can create the experience you wish to have and can do so now at this time or whenever you wish or feel ready.

The universe is constantly expanding and you are expanding with it. Know this so that you can be at peace with your decisions in the world and know that you are always on the right path, no matter what you do.

Day 52

Question:
How can I "surrender" to God and still be myself?

Answer:
There is no need to surrender. There is no one and nothing to surrender to. Trust is the key to your process.

Trust in that place within yourself where your true self resides. It is not a real physical place but since you live in time and space it might be easier to use those words.

Trust in the process in which you can develop a way of acting and thinking that comes from that inner place and not from the thoughts and emotions of your mind.

Trust that everything works out just the way it is supposed to and that you need do nothing to help it along.

Allow thoughts, ideas and actions to come to you rather than making a large effort. These are the ways that trust in your true self develops and grows until it is the only way you think, feel and act.

Day 53

Hear our Voice

This is the voice within and the reason you can hear it so clearly if you wish is that you have cleared the way for your true inner guidance to come to the fore. This is not the same as channeling wherein the person does not have a consciousness that they recognize as they are speaking or writing.

This is a true blending of spirit and a physical body.
This is the way things were meant to be but have been forgotten.

It is false that you are here to be separate from this voice. You are here for the expansion of the experience and as such it is good to have guidance at times, if not at all times, to help you on your path. This voice serves as such until the time comes when you are completely blended with it and there is no separation from it. It is not hard to do. However your habituated way of thinking that you are separate from the vast body of true knowledge that exists keeps you from this blending and abiding as one being.

Until then you hear it as a separate voice. Some call it the Holy Spirit, others their guides and give them names, while still others choose to think of it as their higher self speaking to them. It is one and the same.

Know that no one speaks to you, no one speaks through you. There is information that you can receive but the thinker and the speaker are the real you.

Day 54

You ask yourself, "How can I achieve peace for myself in the world?"

And we answer you, bring the peace of God with you wherever you go, wherever you are. Notice when the little things are upsetting you and stop them in their tracks, calling upon the peace of God to bring you back home where you truly belong. At each moment ask yourself, "Is this the peace I want?" And you shall be free of all the small and petty annoyances, upsets, overwhelments that you think you face.

Tell yourself that you want the peace of God above all else. Ask for help at every turn. Ask for the One within you to help you so you are not acting alone as a separate being. Know that there is always help available for you.

See your fellow man as God would see him, innocent and pure. Love him no matter what. Know that it matters not. Do the best you can do but know that the effort does not have to come from you.

Practice this at all times, or when you remember to do so.

These practices will bring you the peace of mind you seek.

Day 55

Today we will speak with you about faith, how to have faith and trust when the things of the world make you think that you falter.

All is within you. All is encompassed within your loving thoughts.

There is faith in oneself that one will be able to do well. There is faith in something greater than yourself that knows all and is protective of you. You may call this God or higher self or inner teacher or the universe. You may call this fate or the masters or universal mind. It is all one.

Have faith that something outside of your human experience exists that you can touch upon. Trust that all is truly well.

There is only one mind. This is the universal mind. You could say that all thoughts and knowledge, both human knowledge and the knowledge of eternity are stored there. There is no real place and no real storage bin, it is more energetic than that, but let us use this as an example. From that universal mind repository is every thought that has been thought. There is every feeling that has been felt. There is every part of love that exists. When you enter a meditative state and ask for guidance it is from this universal mind and knowledge that your answers will come. In a receptive state you can tap into that ever expanding repository. You can attract those ideas and thoughts to you and expand upon them and add to them if you wish. This is how new things happen. This is how ideas in human consciousness come about. Know that in a receptive state you can know anything you want. It is there for you.

You may pick up on negativity from others but cast it aside because it is not of you. You are only light and love and no matter how the world outside may seem, this is your mission: to be the light and love. Light, however, can pierce through the fog and if you choose to be that kind of light that is good. If you choose to spread the light, that is also good. It is all there for you.

Having faith that you are the light as God is the light is the single most important aspect that you can learn. Your faith that the light will prevail over darkness, that you will not be left in the darkness, alone and separate, is a mantra you can tell yourself over and over. You are not alone, all is within you and you are all. Your mind and the universal mind are one, you and God are one. You are one with all.

Day 56

The creation of the world

Unlike many things you may have read the creation of the world came from the mind of God and the splitting off of the various interests of the mind of God. It did not come from aliens from outer space inserting their DNA into your body. It did not come from a slow evolutionary natural selection process. It did not come from some "tiny mad idea" that you are separate from God and wanted to explore what it would feel like to be separate. These are great illusions which may serve the mind's purpose but are not truth.

You are never separated from God. It cannot be, because you are of a whole, an entirety, and everything is connected to every other thing. There are no exceptions. You are either asleep and unaware of this or you are awake and aware. And it matters not if you are asleep or awake because you are always connected to God.

From the mind and intentions of the energy you know as God came the universe and beyond the universe, this planet and its inhabitants and all other planets and theirs. This planet was created with the intention of exploration of the outside and the inside. It was created for thinking and feeling to be united. Sometimes they are split off but for the most part, if you reflect on this, you will see your thinking and feeling are the same, one leads to the other.

Those of you who would like to transcend this experience and be with God always may do so. You do not have to physically die to do this. But those who choose to just live in the world, experiencing bad and good and not thinking further are truly well also. There is no difference. Everyone is awakened, from the baby to the grandmother, from the beggar to the president of the company. It is just their awareness which makes a change. There is no difference in all of you. It is a matter of degrees of awareness, of presence.

Day 57

The creation of the world, continued

There are many who want to believe that this planet is inhabited by those energies that have come from another planet. This is truly not so. You are of an energy vaster than yourself but those who would like to believe that they are from elsewhere do not feel comfortable in the world and therefore make a nice story for themselves about their origins.

You were created from an idea in the energetic realm. You decided to come here. You decided to play and to cry here. It is all preordained. Your soul has a mission and lessons to learn for its ongoing expansion and for the expansion of the universe. Therefore you choose to have certain experiences which are all for the knowing of this experience. Some ones can understand it while they are in physical bodies here on earth, but the others will understand it soon enough after they leave their bodies. Know that you can be here and know God at the same time. You can love and hate and still be redeemed at the end.

There is no difference in the eyes of God, who has inner vision. You can develop this same inner vision as it is part of you and not separate from you no matter how hard you might seem to try. Know always that you are one with God and that you are both God's creation and your own.

Day 58

Question:
What is hope?

Answer:
Hope in your sense is the anticipation of a better future. Hope leads to disappointment but it seems that people need hope in order to survive their present experience.

True hope, however, is knowledge, the knowledge that all is truly well, that God's will for you on earth is completely known and that by turning toward this higher way of thinking, which is within oneself, one can feel hopeful.

Hope does not need to lead to disappointment, not if hope is seen differently. Think of it more as a way of going about in the world, a way of knowing that you are in the right place, the right time, the right circumstance for you always. Know that there is no fear and no death. Know that within yourself exist all the answers that you seek. Then you can have a sense of hopefulness.

Know that all reach the same goal in their own way, whether during this lifetime or afterward and then you will have a sense of hopefulness about everyone and everything.

Know that you and everyone else chose to be here at this time and place and that all is perfect just as it is and you will have hopefulness.

In this way you can see that there is another meaning to hope. It has nothing to do with wishing present circumstances were better. It has everything to do with the inner knowing that you are already home, heaven on earth, and that all is perfect just as it is.

Day 59

The meaning of love

Love is a universal expression but we are not talking of the love people have for each other, the cloying, possessive, worried love or the ecstatic individual exclusive love. Rather, love for all is what we would like to speak about today.

Love for all is impersonal. Love for all takes you out of this world and its problems, the negative feelings in your mind, and brings you into communion with God and with all that exists. This love is truly all that there is, but it is not just a feeling. It is a state of being. It is a state of being in the moment and being with universal consciousness. It is a state of knowing and observing. It is a state of treating all as equals and seeing the God that is in them at all times.

This universal love takes you into your self and out of it at the same time. It taps into both the little you and the larger picture. Love like this is endless and infinite.

It is the love of God, the love God has for you and everyone else. This love is comforting. This love is wise. This love is the thought in the mind of God that made you and everything else. This love extends itself out forever and never ends, always expanding and moving exponentially into infinity.

This is the love you seek to feel for everyone and everything if you want true peace and understanding.

This love has been misunderstood because it is impartial and impersonal. This love is for the tsunami as well as the victims; it is for the nuclear power and for those who perish because of it. This love made the world and continues to create. It is where creation originates and nowhere else. This love is not only ethereal, it is practical. The love for all is the love that is within your heart. Open to it and see the difference it makes in the way you perceive what surrounds you.

Day 60

The end of the world

There is no end and no beginning.
The physical world as you know it might end at some time when a confluence of physical influences allows that to occur, but that is of no matter.

The world will end when you and your mind are one. It will end when you decide it will. It will end when you decide to explore other universes and experiences.

The end of the world for you is not the end of the world for others. Others may return here over and over again as is their wont. For you who prefer to have experiences and then rest in God's love, at some juncture you will decide to not return. You make that decision just as you make the decision to come here. This is neither something to mourn nor to rejoice. Many souls make this decision at all times. These souls are available to help you while you are here if you and they desire. Call upon them if you wish for we are all one energy.

The world will end for you when you have decided that you are true perfection and there is no longer a need for a physical presence and experience. Then you will join the ranks of souls that decide to have a different experience elsewhere or in the nonphysical realm. You can decide to remain a presence here nonphysically or not. The choice is yours. Always follow your true desire in this regard. You are not being groomed for any great high and lofty "job" in the nonphysical realm. It is all your choice and there are endless possibilities. You never end. Therefore your experiences never end, whether physical or nonphysical. So there is nothing to fear and only endless expansion and exploration. This should be a comfort to you. You never end, you constantly learn and expand, you constantly interact albeit in a different way with the souls of God's creation and you can be as close to God or as far away as you like. It is above as it is below.

The universe within your mind is greater than the one outside it. Continue to expand and you will find what you seek.

Day 61

A Prayer

Let me sit in stillness
The silence surrounds
Darkness is outside
Inside is illumined
Joy and allowing
Love and peace
Let my heart and mind
Abide here as one

Day 62

The Resurrection

There is only one God, there is none else. There may be gods that others worship including Buddha, Jesus, Mohammed, the Goddess, Shiva. But there is only One.

The Oneness is within you and without you. The Oneness is for all to see and experience, however some choose an intermediary. There is no need for intermediaries. There is nothing wrong with them, it is just unnecessary. Jesus, Buddha, these were men who walked on earth just as you do. They were no different except in their questions and the answers they always received. You are one with them. There is no need to worship them as Gods unless you choose to do so. Jesus, Buddha—they both led the way to enlightenment but they did not want to deify themselves.

So on this Easter take the lead from them and do not deify anyone or anything. Worship the truth within yourself. That is all you need.

Day 63

Question:
What is this thing called "No Thought?"
Is it possible to have no thoughts, no thoughts at all?

Answer:
O Holy One,
It depends on how much thought you bring to the table. Perhaps you do not want no thought, you just want "enlightenment." Perhaps you do not want to think negative thoughts but only positive ones. Perhaps you want to be like an animal that supposedly has no thoughts, but you are afraid you will be impulsive like an animal and act before you think.

There is no "no thought." Thoughts always arise or do not arise in the mind. Even those who are "enlightened" have some thoughts. Even if the words come out of their mouths in their teachings or sayings, it is still their thoughts, not someone else's. Even the writing of these words, this is still your thought, not some others.

So the idea of no thought at all—it can be achieved in meditation and stillness, in going about your daily life, in remembering to not think, but for the average person, there are thoughts, lots of them, and it is all right to have them.

The attention you pay to the thoughts, the meaning you give to the thoughts is what gets you into trouble.

There are some, a few, who live in a state of being and of no thought. But that is not most people. To aspire to this when it seems so far away will only bring frustration. Instead focus on no one thought being any more important than any other.

Turn your thoughts toward something else, like God or Oneness. This is the quickest way to stop obsessive thinking and put your mind into rest and stillness. The thought of God, turning toward God, the God within you, is where you can find the most peace. Your definition of God can be whatever works best for you or no definition. Just turn your attention away from the thought, acknowledge it and turn toward God. This is not a distraction. This is a turning toward your true self. And it can work every time.

You will need to climb this ladder until you are always with God, with God's love, and then, the need to turn off the thoughts will dissipate as all thoughts will be focused on God's love. There is nothing else.

Day 64

Go within to find the peace you seek.
As attachments to the world, to others, to yourself fade, they will drift away and you will be still within yourself. You find that this is the state of being from which you view everything, a point of contact with the truth or God which anchors you and fills the space that is you.

Thoughts and feelings come and go and you may be caught in them for a moment, but then you remember, recalling who you truly are.

To be in this state of being, grounded within yourself and the universe, is the most natural state of all. It is just beingness and it is very alive. It is not about your perceptions or thoughts, your feelings or ideas. It is a state beyond consciousness but where you are fully conscious. You need not lose yourself in this since there is no self to lose anyway. It is more a true way of being at all times that you can remember. And as you remember it more, the peace and quiet of this state is with you always.

Allow for now the violence of emotional storms to rage if they must, but know that they need not. There is no longer a need for these feelings to be anything else but a breeze upon the still water, creating a ripple here and there but not disturbing the deep.

Allow that deep stillness to arise no matter what outward circumstance there is. Then there is no thinking, no words, no doing, not even being. "Just being" is much overrated.

There is only Oneness and understanding of all. All the human frailties of oneself and others, which are false and yet so believed, have disappeared.

Day 65

Message of Healing

Do not think that you cannot heal. As you seek the services of doctors, healers and God, you too can decide to heal. If you are contemplating various avenues to pursue, we say to you: every single time you notice, turn toward God for guidance, the God who is completely within you.

Healing starts from the inside to the outside, so the outer signs are the last to go. When they go you have confirmation that you are free. But you must believe and know that you are free of all illnesses before that occurs. It is not a miracle that just happens to you. It is conscious creation by being in the sacred space of the moment.

Whenever there is a symptom, say a word of thanks to the God within for pointing the way toward the truth. Each symptom shows you where the truth really lies. It all comes up to the surface to be healed.

You are more powerful than you can imagine, especially in this realm. It takes a conscious effort to be in that space within and stay there as much as you can. You will see, either gradually or quickly, that you are whole and in balance.

It is true that there are some who feel closer to God once they are ill, it is the way inward for them, but this need not be the case. Have no fear because by turning toward the God within, you can receive the guidance meant for you.

Day 66

We say you can receive enlightenment in an instant or it can take your whole lifetime.
Acceptance is the key.
Accept what is and disregard that which you think might bother you.
Accept everything for what it is without judgments,
Accept and do not push against it,
Then and only then does the wall fall away,
And beyond it is the clearest blue sky,
The wavy field of grain,
The loving laps of the ocean waves.
There does your peace abide.
There you find your true self.

Day 67

There is no death. There is only life, the life of the soul.
So if one chooses to exit the body, it is always by choice.
They sometimes want to renew again, they sometimes want
to end their suffering.
They sometimes feel they have done enough here and want
to be at peace without a body.
But there is no eternal repose.
It is active and moving in a way a body cannot
understand.
It is vivid and transcendent, what you can only get a
glimpse of on earth.
There is no need to go away for this experience,
You are in this experience right here, right now,
You have just forgotten, you have just turned away and
walked in another direction.
So turn again toward where you truly are and want to be.
And the glorious experience you seek, at one with all, is
here.

PART III

ༀ

PRAYERS AND POEMS

Day 68

It is time for rejoicing. Singing and clapping.
It is time for spring to awaken your soul.
Love and desire are in the air.
Ensure that you are there to catch its essence.
Dance and be happy.
Twirl in the fields.
Rejoice in the God that
Gave you life.
Know you are loved in every instant.
The moment is yours.
Take it and run freely.

Day 69

My love for all is a greater love than just for one person
or thing
My love expands to the entire universe
Encompassing everything
It is personal and impersonal
It is free—freely given and freely received
My love for all is greater than I can imagine
I love and I am truly loved
Amen

Day 70

O Holy One
Greet the day in joy.
End the day in rest.
In between find forgiveness for anything else.
Love all those around you and go about your day.
Think not about them,
Rest your gaze on God.
Think not at all,
Stillness is the key.
Through this moment will come
All that you ever need.

Day 71

Affirmations

All is love and light. Bring this pure white light into your presence and your being. You will light up the world.

With God all things are possible. This means let God do the work. You sit back and enjoy the ride.

Trust in the Lord. This means surrender yourself to the higher knowledge that all will always be taken care of. There is no need to worry about anything. Accept all as it is.

Be your true self at all times. Be in touch with the truth within you. It will always be for your greatest good.

Turn it over to God at every moment.

Peace is possible this instant. Turn toward God and you shall find peace.

Let yourself shine and be a light to the world. As the light grows within you, all will see and feel it. In this way you are a true world server and give all to others. You will be continuously replenished. The light is unending, forever.

Day 72

Always know that you are loved
Whether you are in pain or in joy
Soak in the ever-present love of God's light
And be One with everything
Love is the only way
An open heart and a quiet mind
Will lead you within
To the loving arms of God
Where you will be joyful and at peace

Day 73

You have sat in silence for many years
And now your voice is found
Do not think in writing these words that
Your silence is broken
Instead see it as the pure love of God
Pouring out of your fingers
Just as you speak
So do you write
The love of God is all around you
The peace of God surrounds your being
The words of God come from your lips
The mind of God and yours are One

Day 74

O Holy One
Today begin anew
And see that you are completely free
There is no prison that is holding your spirit
There is nothing that hinders you, envelops you or stops
you
Except what you hold in mind
Dissolve all thoughts and listen
Within
The answer to all your questions is the same:
"All things are echoes of the Voice for God"

Hear it today

Day 75

All is One, there is no one else out there but you.
There is no God out there but you.
Nothing is out there, it is all within you,
It is you.
Today in time and space you may see it all as separate,
Separate beings with separate thoughts
But this is an untruth.
If we expand to encompass the entire universe
Then we are all one being, living and breathing together,
In the rhythm of the universe
That you can feel so easily
Only but give it a chance.

Day 76

Bathed in light
It shines out to you
It shines out from you
It is all around
Heavenly sounds
Meld in your mind
A symphony unsung
A bird without a voice
But within
Are worlds
And no-thing
The vast space which is nameless
The collapse of all you know
Dwell in this no-space and no-time zone
You can view everything from this vantage point
And see it for what it is
The workings of the ego, the little self,
The workings of God, the big self,
It is all laid out
But at the beginning and in the end
There is only light
Pure, loving light
Amen

Day 77

The peace and light of God are all you have
There is no separation, only that which is within your mind
Let go of ideas that there is a God and a you
Let go gently or violently, it does not matter
For you will see the light within
As clearly as you see the sun without
No differences to be ascertained
When you are One with all
The darkness is there too, to give you rest and
Let you choose what you truly want
But the light within
Is always bright
You cannot obscure it
It will not extinguish
It burns forever like an
Eternal candle

Day 78

Freedom is what you seek
True freedom is only in the mind
The mind of peace and forgiveness
Let nothing disturb your freedom today
No matter in what situation you may be
Let it go far away
And take counsel within
To that place where no pebble can cause
A ripple
Pray and reflect, be one with it
And your freedom is assured

Day 79

Endless possibilities are before you
Because it has already happened
You just do not know it
No hoping or wishing is needed
No desires or longings belong
Just being here in this moment in time is enough
Just loving whatever comes before you
The world falls away and is replaced
By a deep knowing, a loving understanding
Of nothing and of everything
Stay here a while
Bring this with you whenever you recall
It will give you peace and happiness

Day 80

You are beauteous beyond compare
You are One with all
As the petal of the flower unfolds
So does your mind
The answer deep within
Watch your self disappear
Watch the world around you do so too
And be in that space of harmony
Where there is only light
Then you will be
Just be

Day 81

You are blessed beyond belief
You are at peace and at One with God
You have merged with all that is
There is none else as the prayer so states
Bask in the love of God today
And all days as they become the
Ever present now
Eternity is here for you are no longer
In time
See through the veils and be with all
Rejoice and be free
Rejoice and be as One
No differences, only holiness
And wholeness abounds
Be free today and every day
Free to act with love and light
Be free to express all that is within you
For that is what you are meant to do

Day 82

There is only One
One me and one you
Merged together
Pray for the two to become One
Live it and it shall be
O Holy One
See all as yourself
See yourself as none
Then you shall be true
To your divine nature

Day 83

Write everything as if you were God
Let the words flow with the voice of love
Speak every word as if you are the kind parent
Lovingly looking at your children and knowing
All is well
May every word that comes from my mouth
Be as one with God
Be as if I am home with God
Where we all belong

Day 84

Truth and freedom intertwine
For when you know the truth you must be free
Free of all illusions
Free to be with all
Freedom leads to love
The love of every thing

Be free with love and God
Be in love with all that comes your way

When true to your inner self
The outer will reflect it
And truth shall be known to all

Day 85

Into the light

We are all light
Light is all there truly is
Everything derives from light
Everything is subsumed by light
Into light we are born
Into light we will go

The light is always present
It is we who cloud it from our conscious experience
Be the light
For yourself and others
Be light toward yourself, be forgiving

God's light was the first and is the only light that exists
All else emanates thereof
Each has that light within
It will never go out

Light that dances on the ocean
Let me feel you within me
Let me merge and be at one with light
Let it shine forth from me
As God's emissary
As the light of consciousness which we all share

Day 86

Let me help others as I help myself
Allow me to shine with hope and love
In the loving presence of what is larger than myself
Let all minds be healed in this love
It comes from God and God's presence in us all
Amen

Day 87

My Soul and I are one
United, blended, inseparable
I may seem to be here but I am not
I am just present here
Being and observing
Being all of life
There is nothing to become
There is nothing to do
More than I am already doing

Empty the mind
And find that love for all is within
And all the knowledge of the universe
Is unneeded when that love abounds
Amen

Day 88

I bring silence into the day
The silence of the night when all is still
No rushing thoughts, no rushing bodies
Just a thought of God, the Oneness of us all
The sun is rising, the day begins
A prayer from my lips is all I need

Day 89

Quiet the mind, open to love
Let the sounds of spirit flow through you
In all you say, in all you do
Give up the chatter and outward pretensions
And be your true self, wholly and fully
Be the love that you know you are
To all and every person today
It matters not if you are giving or receiving
Just being you, as the face of God
Is always enough to know love and be loved

Day 90

In this dark moment before the sun arises
I will separate my thinking mind from the day before me
And join with God's voice
The morning rituals only serve to prepare me
For the presence of love
Allow me to merge into that kindness and light
As I stop my thinking mind
And praise the consciousness of love and gratitude
"May the words of my mouth
And the meditations of my heart"
Be One with you always
I am open to receive
The warm and loving embrace of All
Amen

Day 91

Do not thirst for God, although you are in a drought
Do not long for God as if it is a lover wanting to come
home
Do not seek for God, you will not find God there

Just be
At peace
In One
With all

This is the only way to find Me
This is the only way to find yourself
The true self, waiting to reveal
Its shining essence to you

Day 92

A Meditation

Lift the veil
Allow me to see life as it truly is

As the sky is blue, go beyond
Let nothing stop me, let my mind open
To the spaciousness beyond the stars

Look at the leaf and see all of creation
Look at the water and see the universe
Look within and find everything I need

Nothing is there except an empty stillness
Everything is there

Day 93

Be with the One
Free your mind of all other thoughts
Let thoughts gently go
And turn toward God alone

Here is your rest
And here lies all answers
No more questions needed
Only love and devotion

Think only of you
Think only of God
One and the same
This is the space that you seek

Day 94

Out of silence
Comes light
And peace
The root of all causes
God and me

Help me to be
In silence with You
And see no difference
Between us

As I meld into
Your holy light
Bring me acceptance
And love
Amen

Day 95

Be with God
All day and night
There is no one else
So give up your resistance
And see yourself as one
With all that is
Know that there are no thoughts of God
That are not your own
You are the extension
Of that father's love
Embrace it and send it out
To all, to everywhere, to all time

Day 96

When I think of
What God has planned for me
Without even planning
I am filled with joy
The script is already written
The plan is clear—
Be only with God, who is within and without
Be only for God, there is no other way
Do nothing unnecessary
Everything is truly unnecessary
Because it is all already here
If I close my eyes I can see it
If I open my eyes I can live it
Amen

Day 97

I trust in God rather than my self
The small self with fears and needs
I do not do anything by my self
Only with the Oneness of all

I am not a body to be healed
I am not a mind to be changed
I have not eyes to see differently

I am blended not surrendered to the One
And in this I am more than me
But part of a whole so vast
It is unexplained in the world
But in this silence all can be revealed

Day 98

In a moment of wonder
God is there
A prayer is answered
Who else would it be?

Turn toward God
At every moment
And you will open
To the loving arms
That reach within
And offer all you will ever need

It is simple and kind
And yet
It is hard to remember
Who you really are

Just be love
The rest always follows

The light of God shines through you
It surrounds you
It is unending
And it is you

Day 99

Nothing more is needed
All has already occurred
We live parallel
To all our other experiences

Be at peace
That you will always choose
What is your right path

You will never be led astray
It is not possible

Trust in God and your knowing
That you and God are One

Day 100

All is well
The Sun is in the sky
God is everywhere
The earth is at my feet
I feel the presence
Of all and every piece
That makes up the whole
Greater than I can imagine
Peace surrounds me
Light surrounds me
Love surrounds me
I pray that all who are present
Find this peace that I feel now
It is ready for us all
Open to it, light the way
And it is here
Within you and without
A beauty unsurpassed
Stillness speaks to all
And creates heaven on earth

About the Author

Irene A. Cohen, M.D. is a psychiatrist, acupuncturist and interfaith minister who has maintained an integrative practice for almost 30 years. After completing the Voice for Love program, she began listening to and writing from a clear inner voice, which some would call the higher self or Holy Spirit. Over the past 17 years she has offered workshops on qigong, meditation, color and sound and served on the Emotional Freedom Technique (EFT) Advisory Board.

A native New Yorker, Dr. Cohen now resides in Austin, Texas with her husband Michael Nill

Website: www.drirenecohen.com.